Memoirs of an Ordinary Woman

Volume I

Contains the Stories:

My Brother, Myself

Sex and Satan

&

Poetry

By
The1Essence

Memoirs of an Ordinary Woman, Volume I

Second Edition
First Printing

ISBN-13:
978-0615530123 (The1Essence_Presentations)

ISBN-10:
0615530125

The1Essence Presentations

All character's and incidents contained in this story as a whole, or as separate entities are completely fictional. Any similarity to any persons or events, known or unknown to the author at the time of publication are purely coincidental.

Table of Contents

Teacher

I saw the silhouette of the sun hidden behind the
clouds.
Life looked pale and cold with only sad tales to be
told.
Love,
Sitting beside me said "close your eyes".
Love,
Took my hand and spoke these words,
"tell me the last thing your mind allowed you to
see."
"The grass", I said, "beneath me".
Love continued,
"Where did it come from?"
"How did it begin?"
"Think", Love said,
"Let it come from within".
I began to unwind,
As Love revealed to me
my sins.
"What is this" Love sang, "I've placed in your
hand?"
My mind immediately blurted out, "a single grain of
sand!"
"Try again", Love demanded.
"You've been given a precious gift."
As the endless stream of warm sand slid through my
fingers,
from my hand,
Love began to cry "you've touched all these lives!"
It was then Love begged me "please open your
eyes!"
Slowly,
I began to look around.
Surprising only myself when I began to see the
sunrise…

Memoirs of an Ordinary Woman, Volume I

This book is especially dedicated to my maternal Great Aunts: Dessie, Leslie, Jean, Eula, Dattie, Dorothy and, Mary, my honorary Great Aunt.

God in "Me"

I dream about the day,
when you will come swoop me away.
You're not on a beautiful white horse,
nor,
does your amour gleam.
But,
there are lights dancing all around you,
they're blinding.
Like magnificent sun beams,
your presence brings with it an imposing force;
that announces to all,
you're my right choice.
You fill my mind and body with an ultimate glee,
And in return you only ask that "I" be "Me".
A "Me" that blends perfectly with "U",
creating harmony through Love,
that defines the word true.
Thank-you my Knight,
for bringing with you the day,
that joy shined on us,
a light to last always.
With it washing my dreams away,
giving life to a generous reality,
filled with God's Grace.
Thank-you Sweet Prince,
for showing me the difference between reality and
real life.
Then, making them one in the same.

Memoirs of an Ordinary Woman, Volume I

Acknowledgements

Robert Blalock
James Blalock

Sunshine

On this day
The sun shines
On my face
And I no longer
Think my past
Was a waste
Understanding
Life
Is really not
A race
But
Meant to be
Lived
With as many
Smiles
As I can muster
Realizing
Our experiences
Together
Were the best
At that time
A lesson offered from
Above
Learned
Now its time to move on
Remembering yesterdays
With a smile
While
Looking forward to
More sunshine
Inside
My tomorrows

MY BROTHER, MYSELF

Every so often the memories of my brother weigh heavily on my mind. Many times I find myself praying for his soul's redemption and wondering if I had the chance to do things differently, could I?

There were times when life afforded me the opportunity to be a selfish and spoiled child, and later the same as a young woman; surrounded by loved ones who only wanted the best in life for me; pacified by love that warmed my heart and soul as any child should feel. My brother is one in my life who stands out as a constant provider of that type of love.

Even now, when we are separated by what can be considered as life, I remember the times when lifestyles selfishly kept us apart. A fault shared by the both of us.

First and foremost, I must explain the relationship. You see, my brother, biologically is not my bother.

Growing up, my mother often performed disappearing acts. We didn't know it then, but she was later to be diagnosed as clinically bipolar, unable to emotionally care for herself; let alone a child. Her actions were dismissed as unstable and accepted her "condition", as done in most Black families.

It was during the times when my mother disappeared that I would live with her maternal aunt and family; the Jenkins. In this home, I experience a sense of what most people define as a normal family.

Although later in life I learned we were far from normal.

Here I had a father, mother, two older brothers and two older sisters. I was the youngest and denied nothing my heart desired, showered with undying affection and attention no matter the occasion. Here I was the center of attention, and happy with the title.

Of my two brothers, Robert is the youngest. He is my second cousin and elder by 10 years. But, you couldn't tell either one of us the cousin part was truth. Our hearts were bonded as if genetics didn't exist. He is my teacher and, my protector.

I don't remember too much about our early years together. Memories of that time are very faint. But, I do have stories that are passed around the Jenkins household whenever I cross their threshold, like candy during Halloween.

I went to live with the Jenkins's at the age of six months; at the end of a family feud to determine who would care for the 15 year olds child and, after living with at least three other relatives, in two different states.

Ruby Jenkins, to whom I still affectionately refer to as mom, is my grandmother's sister and married to Henry Jenkins who will forever remain my daddy in this life or otherwise, despite who my actually father is.

Then there was Thomas, my oldest sibling, followed by Theresa or Reese, Robert and then Brianna.

The spoken plan was to return me to my mother upon her graduation from high school. But, no one knew the bond between me and my surrogate family would grow so strong.

You see, back in those days, most Black families still subscribed to the now defunct adage of it taking a village to raise a child, whereas now, most Black children are raising themselves.

I was immediately welcomed into the household.

Daddy worked at a local factory and mom was a domestic. All of us children had our place and responsibilities in the home. Well, let me rephrase that. All of the older children had responsibilities in the home. And, the main responsibility after my arrival was taking care of me.

Each took turns babysitting until mom got home from work. I am told that this was the cause of many arguments because at that time they were all young adults trying to carve their notch in life. And realistically, who has time for a new baby at that age?

I don't know if Robert was ever delegated that responsibility initially and, that is not a matter of importance for me at this point. Yet, I'm sure there is a story about that which someone hasn't told.

My first solid memories of Robert begin when I was six. I had been given back to my mother at the age of two and with much controversy.

Mom, I am told even had a stroke the day my mother came to stake her permanent claim to me, which was immediately after her high school graduation.

Until then, I had been raised being told and believing that my mother was my cousin. Can you imagine the shock for such a small child? Believe me that is the subject of another memoir and the source of much of the insecurity I carry with me today.

This wasn't the first time, or the last I was back "home". My mother couldn't seem to get a grip on what she wanted or who she wanted in her life. Yes, another memoir and more insecurity for me.

By this time, Thomas and Theresa were all grown up and out on their own. Thomas had met and married a beautiful Puerto Rican woman named Marisol and, Theresa had her own place but, no particular love interest.

Home was a tiny three bedroom bungalow house in back of a larger duplex on 14th and Keefe, which sat with its rear bordering an alley.

Milwaukee is one of the most unique cities I've lived in due to the fact that all the older neighborhoods had alleys. Which, even today are the harbors of wrong doings.

Robert had begun hanging out with his friends, who weren't up to much good, on a regular basis, often until well after his curfew; only to come home to a whooping administered by daddy, yelling or the threat of punishment.

I would hear these things going on downstairs, when I was supposed to be sleeping but, I was waiting on him to come home too. I often found myself thinking that if I were to run downstairs and cry it would stop the controversy, and we could go back to being a happy, somewhat normal family. But, I never once got up to interfere, mainly, because I didn't want to risk getting a whooping also.

I had never been whooped in that household. In fact, I had never even been spanked (yes there is a difference in Black families), only threatened by mom and my siblings when I would get out of hand. Daddy only gently reprimanded me when I would interrupt his concentration during whatever sports he was watching, otherwise he only had hugs and kisses for me, and an occasional dollar to stop the tears no matter how out of hand I had gotten.

Robert was upset about things I was unaware of at the time and acting out. First and foremost, daddy had a mistress and it got worse.

Apparently, it had been revealed to the rest of the family that daddy had another family with his mistress, with the same number of children and close to the same age as all of mom's children, all his. Daddy had a good job but, not good enough to support two families with children numbering eight, and that didn't include me.

Of course, he supported them both and, because my mother couldn't or wouldn't support me financially (if she did, that is another family secret) he had to bear the monetary weight of us all. Then again, why shouldn't he? This was his mess.

Mom still worked as a domestic but, it there was never enough money most months to make ends meet. Robert thought his mother deserved better and began to harbor resentment towards daddy for our living conditions and above all hurting his mother.

Unbeknownst to me, at that time, daddy was beating on mom and most likely the beating were the result of an argument regarding his whereabouts and his affair. And, I began to have nightmares.

These nightmares happened during times when I wasn't alert enough to wait on Robert or Brianna to come home. Let's just say I was a heavy sleeper. Being happy and content can do that to you.

I learned later that during these fights were the only times I would have nightmares and, it was always the same nightmare.

Three stones in a brook, the size ranges were large, medium and small, like in the story about the three bears. The water in the brook would be running full force, but it wasn't deep enough to cover the stones. Then suddenly, without warning, the large stone would pop up and fall viciously on top of the medium stone and then the both of them would fall even harder onto the small stone. This created a feeling of suffocation and massive suppression in my chest.

I would wake up screaming, believing someone was trying to suffocate me and mom would come up to comfort me and put me back to sleep. Hey, I told you I was spoiled at times. After the nightmare, I would always sleep peacefully.

Robert knew what was going on between his parents. Everyone knew everyone that is except me. I wasn't supposed to know. I was supposed to focus on school and church.

Church was the most important because daddy was on the deacon board. And everyone knows, in a Black Baptist church, the deacon's family should be the most proficient in their lessons. They are also, normally, along with the pastor's children, the most notoriously defiant.

Robert began selling weed in small amounts to help mom make ends meet. But, his ultimate goal was to save up enough money to get her out of that neighborhood and buy her a house.

At first mom and daddy didn't know about it. But, when Robert began coming home later and later with clothes they didn't buy, then locking himself in his room, they were alert enough to put the pieces together. By then, he had stopped going to school and church completely.

Hanging out with his friends doing only God knows what, was the obvious priority but, Robert had bigger plans for his new occupation.

On the occasions when he was delegated to babysitting me he became my confidant. I would tell him what went on with me during his absence. Rambling on and on about school church or what Brianna got in trouble for, while he would patiently listen as he removed the seeds and packaged his product. Only responding with, "mmmhum" or a nod until I had exhausted myself or his nerves talking a mile a minute.

Then he did what any teenage brother would do in that situation; told me to be quiet for a while; but, never shut-up. If I was able to control myself long enough for him to regenerate his patience, he would offer advice for anything he thought was a problem or just contemplate on what he wanted in life for himself or me.

He even let me go over my homework, bible study or just read to him sometimes. But, as soon as mom or Brianna came home, usually Brianna because mom worked late most days, he was out. That didn't bother me because Brianna let me talk until I got tired of talking to her.

The day came when Robert formally became my protector; Curt had come to live with us. Curt was the son of daddy's favorite cousin, whose wife had recently died.

He was going through sort of a troubles and couldn't deal with raising Curt, a teenager who wanted to be a "bad boy", alone. Curt most often got in trouble while his dad working his third shift job and could not be monitored, so mom and dad took him in too.

I'm going to be honest with you. At first I loved having Curt around. He would play with me, read to me and help me with my studies just like Robert would. Only he didn't have the freedom Robert and Brianna did and was around more often than not.

Boy, did I give him a hard time just for the fun of it. On one occasion I was supposed to go to a birthday party. Mom had told Curt that I wasn't supposed to go anywhere until I had eaten (back then, it was embarrassing for your child to appear hungry to others), but I was too excited to eat and just wanted to get to the party.

Normally I could manipulate Curt to just letting me do what I wanted to do and he would get in trouble, not me. But this day was different, he was being difficult.

Mom had given the order that, if I didn't eat (I was always a light eater), I wasn't supposed to go. If she found out differently, Curt would pay for it.

At first, he tried to be authoritative and make me eat. I wasn't going for that. I wined that I wasn't hungry. Then he pleaded for me to eat so that he could drop me off at the party and go hang out with his friends. That didn't work either.

I defiantly said "no, I don't care about your dumb friends".

Finally I realized that I was going nowhere without eating.

I had to figure a way out without having to eat at home. Besides, there would be hotdogs and chips at the party.

I wasn't allowed to eat those things at home, and I sure wasn't going to miss the opportunity, I really had to think this thing out. Then, I remembered Reverend Beauchamp's sermon from previous Sunday.

Of course at the age of seven, the true meaning of his sermon was way over my head but, it would serve its purpose none the less. So, I set my plan in motion. I went to the refrigerator picked out an apple, sat the table and began to eat it.

Curt was in the kitchen on the phone and immediately began to fuss at me, "girl that ain't food! Momma said you had to eat what she cooked!"

I shouted back "no she didn't, she just said I had to eat something and she knows I don't like pig feet anyway!"

The war of intelligence had begun,
"You need to eat some meat!"

My plan was unfolding perfectly as I said, "this *IS* meat".

"Dumb girl" he snapped back "that is fruit, not MEAT!"

He thought he had me but, now, it was time to reveal that I was in fact much smarter than he,

"This apple has meat IN it! Reverend Beauchamp said on Sunday that we have to focus on the MEAT of the FRUIT! So, either you are telling me he's the dumb one or this apple has meat in it!"

Checkmate! He just stood there with his mouth open for a few seconds while I continued to chomp on the apple, then laughing he said

"Finish your apple so that we can get out of here smarty pants!"

This scene was the source of laughter in our family for many years. I never got yelled at and, fortunately for Curt, after relaying the story to mom, daddy and anyone else who would listen to it, he didn't get in trouble either *and*, I got to eat my hotdogs and chips!

One night Curt stopped being fun to be around.

Everyone was out for various reasons and he had the task of babysitting me. This was not an unusual thing and I was very comfortable with it.

Curt made sure I had eaten the dinner mom left for us to eat, did my homework, took a bath and made it to bed by my bedtime. Normally, after I had gone to bed he took to the phone, laughing and trying to sweet talk his love interest of the week. Tonight, was strangely different. There were no phone conversations after I went to bed.

Instead he took a bath and came into the now dark room I shared with Brianna. This didn't initially bother me because he would often come in there to get "something". This was before I had any knowledge of rape, incest or molestation. I was about to get a crash course.

Curt didn't move to Brianna's side of the room. He stood above my bed with only his bath towel on. I thought he was going to yell at me for not cleaning out the bath tub or something but, instead, in this really weird tone told me to "move over".

Today, I can't explain why I did it other than I really was sheltered and had no idea of what was getting ready to happen.

As he slid beside me, he removed his bath towel and whispered "do you know what sex is?"

I was getting scared now. Now, I began to feel something wasn't right. I knew what sex was and I knew it was what married people did to make babies. Why was he asking me that question, and why did he take his towel off? I didn't respond. Then he leaned over and kissed me on the cheek

"Have you ever had sex before?"

Thinking he would immediately leave if I answered, I told him "no".

He grabbed my hand and began to move it toward what I knew as his private parts. I resisted and he forced my hand to touch him.

"Touch it for me, please".

"NO! GET OUT OF HERE OR I'M GONNA TELL ON YOU", I yelled! But, there was no one else at home to hear me.

"Shhhhh! Be quiet, this won't take long", he whispered.

What did he want? Why wouldn't he go away? Then, I thought to myself, "if I just touch it, he will leave". But, he didn't. He took his fingers and began to pull at what was then defined as my "pocketbook". It hurt and I started to cry,

"Just pull on it for me, I won't tell on you, cause I can tell you're not a virgin".

Virgin?? What the heck was he talking about?? I wasn't doing anything that I would get in trouble for. And, I didn't remember getting married so, there was no way that I couldn't have been a virgin! This was very wrong.

"If you don't get outta my bed I am going to tell momma and daddy as soon as the get home" I yelled!

Then God intervened. Suddenly we heard the front door open downstairs and he jumped up to leave. Just as he reached the doorway he whispered "if you tell anyone, I will say you asked me to do it to you".

Then he went back into the bathroom across the hall. I was really scared then. If I told on him, I would get in trouble for being "bad" and "nasty". I didn't know what to do but, I knew what he did was wrong.

The footsteps coming up the stairs told me it was either Robert or Brianna who came home. Mom and daddy very rarely came upstairs. If all was quiet, they knew I was in bed and everything was okay.

When I realized it was Robert who came home, I began to wonder if I could at least tell him what happened. But, the stigma associated with being a nasty little girl was too great. And, how could I live if my brother felt that way about me? So, I just lay there, praying that Curt wouldn't lie to Robert on me, and I determining that I would keep "our" secret and wondering what to do if he tried to do "it" again.

Robert knocked on the bathroom door "did Stacy get to bed on time? That girl never wants to get up in the morning".

Curt mumbled something back and Robert did his usual, going into the room they now shared and shutting the door. I heard Curt come out of the bathroom a short while later and join him.

Just as I started drifting off, I heard Curt laughing and talking to Robert. Almost immediately I heard a loud thud and Robert began yelling.

"What the fuck did you just say? You did what? Motherfucker I will kill you if you ever try that shit again! What the fuck is wrong with you?"

There were more thuds that followed and I heard Curt whimpering something. Then it got quiet and their bedroom door slammed.

I lie there briefly thinking, "What just happened"?

The door to my room slowly opened and Robert called my name asking if I was sleep. I couldn't answer him because the thought hit me that Curt had "told" on me.

Why, did he do that? I wasn't going to say anything!

He came to the bed, leaned over and kissed me on my wet cheek. I didn't realize until then that I had been crying. He sat down on the bed and began to rub my back and talk to me as if he knew I was still awake.

"If that motherfucker ever tries to put his hands on you again, you tell me and that bitch will disa-fuckin-peer! No one, especially family is supposed to touch you that way. He is not your brother, he is not your family, don't ever let him touch you again, in any way. Not even hold your hand when he takes you across streets. If he does, I swear, I'll kill him".

With that said he kissed me on my cheek again and left the room. I felt safe again. I trusted and believe that he would protect me forever.

Shortly thereafter, Robert stopped coming home completely. I'd heard through Alicia and Bryson, Thomas's children that he moved out because mom and daddy found his drugs and threw him out. They knew everything I didn't, largely because Thomas and Marisol talked about anything in front of them.

I loved visiting Thomas's house because there I found out all the juicy family gossip and I would get to do things I couldn't at home, like walk with them to the corner store and to the playground without any supervision. They hardly led the sheltered life that I did when I was with the Jenkins's.

Their daddy beat their mom too, and in front of them at that! They, they also knew their mom and daddy did drugs, and that they bought them from Robert most of the time.

Eventually, my mother came back from her hiatus to claim her possession once again. And, once again I was whisked away from my family.

During the preceding years that totaled 8 in all, Robert and I had sporadic meetings during visits to the Jenkins household. I was well aware of his rising status in the local drug trade by this time, and, benefited from it occasionally.

Robert fully believed in helping those he loved but, he wasn't about to give anyone anything. You had to work for any monies he gave you. He was running what can be called a family business.

Everyone in the family knew about it but, only spoke of in with other family members and everyone tried to get their piece of the pie. And, I mean everyone.

Once I started high school, my mother and my personality conflicts exploded. I ended up living with another one of my grandmother's sister's. The Jenkins home was deemed unfit to raise an impressionable young lady for reasons I respect very much to this day.

Robert had finally been able to buy his mom a house in a better neighborhood but home life would never be the same. You see, all of the Jenkins children had negative life issues working against them.

Thomas, whose wife left and, divorced him by now, was in and out of the jail system and addicted to drugs. He was so horrible that no one in the family would allow him in their home. So, the only home he had left was jail.

I don't know what happened to Marisol after the divorce but, Bryson and Alicia went to live with daddy and mom. They became part of the generation that began raising themselves. Sure, we all still congregated after church on Sunday but, again, it just wasn't the same.

Theresa, who had a stable job and a steady boyfriend had begun her own family and didn't come around much. It's anyone's guess what the problem was there but, at least she was stable.

Robert had his up and coming empire to manage and, had recruited most of the male family members around his age to work for and with him.

And, Brianna, who had recently gave birth a beautiful little girl, was trying to make things work with her baby's father but, was into a little more drama than a new mother should be. Still, I managed to get over there any chance that I could.

I could still do whatever I wanted too when I was there. Mom and daddy were very rarely home so, Bryson, Alicia and I would get into mischief trying to follow behind the 2-4 boys. A gang named for the street most of the members lived on.

Bryson was too little and sniveled to join, I was to "proper" to be inducted but Alicia eventually became a member of the 2-4 Bankettes, the female version of the gang.

We would go to all night skates. Have friends over to the wee hours of the morning or run errands for other family members in the business. Like pick up dirty laundry and dry cleaning.

Robert had invested some of his earnings in a little club called the Sparklin' Ruby. Above the club was his apartment.

I have no idea where the name came from. But, it turned out be a very successful and popular spot. The main customers were people who wanted to buy drugs, pimps, which Robert dually added to his resume, and whores.

Still for a young adult it was fun, when we were allowed to come in. It was all exciting, and taboo to me because I was still be "extra" sheltered.

It was around this time that Robert found out I could iron exceptionally well. A chore I still dread severely to this day. But, I did it then to earn money.

The great aunt with whom I lived then only gave out two dollars, every other Sunday. I think that was allowance but, I was supposed to put most of it in church. So, being in high school, I really needed the money I earned from ironing.

One day, I was visiting the Jenkins household and Robert stopped by. He had a load of laundry an asked Alicia to wash the clothes and then iron them. If she did a good job, he said he would give her 25 dollars. Well, Alicia who didn't have the cash flow problems I had turned him down flat!

I couldn't believe it, 25 dollars? She was crazy! Too much work she said. So, I opened my big mouth and volunteered to take on the job. Like I said, I needed the money and I knew he wasn't going to just give it to me.

Washing the clothes wasn't a problem at all. But, it turned out there were 6 pair of jeans in the bunch to be ironed. My war with the iron was just beginning!

Well, back in the early 80's ironing jeans with an extra sharp crease was very important to the well-dressed pimp. So, I set out to do a spectacular job with hopes to having this as one of my regular gigs.

And, it worked. Robert was so impressed with the crease in those jeans he stopped sending them to the cleaners with his expensive clothes to be starched and started paying me 30 dollars a week to do his wash and wear laundry. After such a long separation, I got to see and talk to him once a week, the money was icing on the cake!

We took full advantage of the time to rekindle our relationship. We talked for what I felt were hours on end. I even taught him a dance or two to do at the club!

Eventually, Robert was arrested and went to jail for a short time and our visits ended abruptly, again. I became preoccupied with finishing high school and boys of course. I never took the time to write him while he was away. How selfish and stupid of me.

While he was gone his parents kept the club open and his crew kept the other business going. The Feds couldn't take it because it was in someone else's name.

A few months before I graduated high school, Robert was released from prison. I didn't find it necessary to visit him when he got home. I was like I said, preoccupied with me.

One day, the week before graduation, I finally paid him a visit at his apartment above the Sparklin' Ruby. I wanted something and I knew there was no way he would deny me.

When I got there, he was seemed very happy to see me. We talked about life, the business; his business as if our relationship had never been interrupted.

Robert schooled me on the pimp game. It's origins and how to spot a trick and a whore, who was making money and who was "false flagin" or "frontin" about making money and being down with the game and gangs.

I paid close attention because I knew one, he wouldn't lie to me and two, he was telling me so I wouldn't fall prey to any of them. In one afternoon, I learned more about the street than I wanted to know. Including what was going on with my Brianna.

Now, I had heard rumors about her dancing, turning tricks and doing drugs. I had even heard that Robert knew about it and that her then boyfriend was her pimp with Robert's blessings.

I couldn't believe that. How many times had family members spread rumors about other family members that were vicious lies? To me this was just another.

Towards the end of my visit, we began to discuss my current living situation and my plans after high school. I had a few cords that were to be worn during graduation around my gown. They had been given to me for various school activities I had participated in.

I don't remember why but, I just happened to have them with me. I gave them to Robert. He was so proud. He hung them around a picture he had hanging over his couch so everyone could see them when they entered his apartment. His little sister was growing up and doing things the right way, in spite of her surroundings. He was very proud.

At some point his pager went off and he had to make a phone call at the pay phone down the street. We walked downstairs to the club together then he left to make the call saying he would be right back and not to leave.

I wasn't going anywhere because I still hadn't told him the purpose of my impromptu visit. He knew I wanted something but seemed not to care.

It was getting late in the afternoon and a few patrons began to trickle in. Brianna and her new beau came in and a couple of cousins followed. Everyone was so happy to see me. They all knew what I had been through with my mother and wanted to let me know they would always be there if I needed them.

I hugged and kissed Brianna. She was petite and very beautiful. I commented on how pretty her dress was then walked a few feet to the bar to get a soda.

At the bar I had begun talking to my uncle Cal when all of a sudden I heard a smack and Brianna fell to the floor crying loudly. No one moved.

I turned around to see her boyfriend standing over her about the hit her again. I jumped off the bar stool and started towards them. No one and I mean no one was going to hit my sister in front of me. My uncle grabbed my arm.

"What in the hell do you think your little ass is going to do?" he asked. "That's their business. She got herself into it and Robert says she's got to get herself out of it."

I stayed put. Shortly, Brianna and her boyfriend and moved their altercation to the upstairs apartment and I could hear her wailing uncontrollably.

I couldn't believe it so I asked my uncle "Robert knows about this" even though he had just told me so.

Now, mind you, I had just sat through half a day of street training and I realized what was going on. The rumors were true!

Turns out Brianna had been given a certain amount of drugs to hold by her boyfriend and when he asked her for them she didn't have them. She was a junkie, a whore and had to be dealt with accordingly.

Noooooo, no, no! Robert would never let something like this happen to Brianna, Theresa or me. He couldn't know.

Robert came back into the bar about 20 minutes later. He smiled when he saw that I was still there and asked what it was that I'd waited so patiently to tell him.

As he sat down on a bar stool next to me the look on my face must have let him know something was wrong. He worriedly looked next at my uncle behind the bar who recalled the traumatizing scene to him, and then Robert turned to me.

"Baby girl," he started, "this life is hard and cold without all the bullshit being in the game brings with it. Brianna mad a choice. Everyone including myself, tried to talk her out of it. You know I wouldn't let my baby sister get so deep in this shit. But, no one could stop her".

"I would rather have this type of shit going on right here in front of me where I can somewhat control things than have her back out on the streets, where I don't know where she is, what she is doing or who she is with. I was mad enough to kill when she ran off with that otha shady nigga while I was locked up".

"But, what could I do? By the time I got home she was already deep into her habits. Here, I can watch her."

What he said next shattered my psyche and eventually pushed me away from my entire family for a short time.

"Baby girl, remember what I told you upstairs? About there are some women that need to be controlled?" I remembered the lesson clearly.

"Well Baby Girl, she's the type of woman I was talking about".

Even today, I remember it like it was this morning. And, it hurts. I was angry. I wanted to walk out of that bar and never speak to any of them again.

They were all losers and I would never be like them.

My fragile sense of security had been shattered. Robert had lied to me. He told me he would always protect me. But, if he wouldn't do it for Brianna, why would he do it for me?

I hated them all for showing me the harshness of life so brutally. But, I was truly awake now. The lessons that afternoon were definitely life lessons. Ones I will never forget. The most important lesson of the day for me was that there was absolutely no one I could trust.

I was angry. I wanted to walk out of that bar and never speak to any of them again. Loving each other was supposed to keep stuff like this from happening.

Yet, I was still selfish and had not received what I had come for. So, I softly said, "ok big brother" and held all the emotions inside. Now, I felt it imperative to let him know my main reason for being there that day.

"Robert, next week after graduation, can I bring a few friends here to party?"

"Girl, is that what you've waited all this time to ask? Of course you can. But, ya'll gotta be outta here by curfew."

I feigned a slight smile.

I should have been happy. A lot of my friends from school lived in the same neighborhood as the bar, knew its repetition and thought it was the place to be. But, I was hurt.

I kissed Robert on the cheek smiled again, "thanks, gotta go" and made a quick exit.

All the way home I could only think of how he had betrayed us all. Women in general, he was supposed to protect us!

As a matter of fact, everything that he was doing was wrong. He was the root of all the problems in the community. A drug dealer, a pimp, and I decided that I would never speak to him again but, not until after my party.

The word got out at school that someone was having a party at the Sparklin' Ruby fast! People I didn't even invite showed up and were surprised that I was the owner's little sister who the party was being given for.

Earlier during the week, I had put my selfishness to work and visited Brianna at mom and dad's house. I told her I had nothing to wear and she loaned me a brand new designer suit to wear.

Robert let us start coming in at 8:30. By 10:00 the place was packed with its regular patrons and the kids from school.

All of my friends felt like royalty as the DJ announce those Madison High School graduates I had invited over the microphone. People I didn't even invite showed up and were surprised that I was the owner's little sister who the party was being given for. We were having the time of our lives pretending to be down.

An older man, much older, asked me to dance. I cringed, because I knew Robert, his crew and other relatives were watching me intensely. If this man made any improper moves, I knew he would "disappear".

I'd heard horror stories spread around the family about Robert's not so gentle side. And, if the rumor about Brianna yielded true, why weren't they?

I looked towards the D.J. booth where my uncle Cal nodded that it was ok. That man danced so much I thought I was going to fall out.

Glancing up towards the stairway I say Robert standing there. He sent one of his crew to tell the man to sit down after we'd danced to four fast songs.

I was glad for that all my friends were have a great time. No one left early and at midnight Robert and his crew descended down the stairs and ushered us out.

We headed to the beach talking about the events of the night. I was on cloud nine and truly the bell of the ball that night!

A couple of months after graduation, the police raided the Sparklin' Ruby and the Jenkins home. They completely tore both places up.

Mom's bedroom door had been knocked of and her safe removed. Robert was jailed and the Sparklin' Ruby seized and shut down for good.

I shrugged it off as just deserved. My heart was hardened towards Robert even though he'd always gone out of his way to be good to me.

Selfishly, that didn't move me. As far as I was concerned it his actions were part of the long con's he'd discussed with me that tragic day in his apartment. Now, to me, he was only a low life drug dealer who had to pay his debt to society. I was never going to be like that.

Mark and I had plans. Although I had been offered a full scholarship to a college in upper Michigan, I was preparing to go into the Army (another stupid decision).

Mark was a freshman at the prestigious Marquette University and he wanted to get married (another dumb move) and raise a perfect family. Just how stupid and naive was I?

Well, a year after graduation Mark and I did get married.

Robert was in Federal prison and he and I hadn't spoken since graduation night. I was trying to be better than all that and not really communicating with most members of my family. There were too many rumors, too many lies and too much drama for me.

A year and a month after we were married, Mark and I welcomed baby number one, a beautiful, healthy and happy little girl and, I was one month shy of my 20th birthday. I sent hundreds of pictures of her to Milwaukee to family member and friends alike.

We had relocated to Ft. Rucker Army Base in Alabama. I was in the Army and Mark was attending the University of Alabama.

We lived on post in NCO housing and anyone on the outside looking in thought we were happy. Things were just the opposite, many nights I wished Robert would make Mark "disappear".

I cried for the big brother that vowed to always be there for me. I needed to be protected from my husband and I needed my big brother to rescue me.

I would never say such a thing aloud. I was too much of a "lady" for that sort of thing, and I know I was wrong for even thinking it. Besides, I was still looking down my nose at him for hurting me. Using his chosen profession as the excuse to stay clear of him, and I absolutely refused to write him.

But, I wanted him in my life so badly. I missed us so much.

About a month after my daughter was born, I received a package in the mail. This being pre 9-11, there was no need for a return address.

It was a medium sized boxed wrapped in plain brown paper and addressed to my daughter. Knowing it was most likely from a family member I paid no attention to where it could have come from and opened it.

Inside was a beautiful pink knitted sweater with pom-pom ties and a matching muffler for the baby's hands, it was beautiful.

Now, my attention turned to where this amazing gift could have possibly come from. And, there stamped on the back of the wrapping was a stamp that read "this package was mailed from a federal correctional facility". ROBERT! Oh my goodness!

He knew about the baby! There was no card, simply the sweater. I wondered if knitting was part of his rehabilitation in prison and he'd made the sweater himself. After a moment or two I quickly dismissed that as viable. He was well liked by too many people, had too much money and, that was just too corny for him. In later years, my uncles would tease me that maybe he did make it himself.

I wanted to thank him. I didn't know where to write. So, I placed a called to mom and discussed the situation with her. I didn't tell her about all the mixed emotions and hurt feelings. I just talked about the sweater and my surprise to receive it.

Mom told me that she'd kept Robert update on my statuses so he knew of my daughter's arrival. She confirmed that the sweater was from him, and that he was very proud of me, then she gave me an address to write him.

Immediately after our conversation I sat down and wrote him a letter and included pictures of my new family. Again, I didn't bother with my hang ups.

I wanted the letter to be as happy and upbeat as possible so, I didn't include the problems I was having in my marriage. I mailed it off with a light spirit, knowing that he was thinking of me just as I was of him. Robert never wrote back but, I didn't care. I knew he loved me just the same as always.

My daughter was two years old when I got out of the military. I pressured my husband to move back to Milwaukee despite his misgivings on the idea.

We were still having problems. No, that was an understatement. We were having major problems. I told him that the reason I wanted to be back in Milwaukee was because I felt it was a great place to raise a family, and I really did think that. But, the main reason was that I needed to be near my family. The fights had gotten more intense and I need their support in any way they could give it to me.

Robert was released from jail a year after we moved back. I found out because he was staying with mom and daddy and just happened to be there one day when I called. He actually answered the phone and I was shocked!

It had been so long since I heard his voice but, we recognized each other right away. Still, the conversation was very strained. I didn't know what to say to him and I was afraid he'd gone back to his old way of life.

We ended our conversation with me promising to bring my daughter to mom and daddy's house to see him. They were still living in the same home he'd bought mom.

I knew when I hung up the phone that I would never fulfill that promise. Robert had made lots of enemies and I didn't want my daughter to be hit by a stray bullet. Or be identified as someone he loved and kidnapped. Yes, I was spacing out and going far left with it but, at the time I found a way to justify it within myself.

Today, it remains one of my biggest regrets. Two more years went by before we communicated again. And, once again he was at mom and daddy's when I called.

By this time it was well spoken of within the family that Robert went back to the only way of life he knew, the streets. I was definitely not trying to run into him for any reason.

My fear of something dreadful happening to me or a member of my family was strong. My marriage was improving and I didn't want anything to interrupt my happiness.

This time the conversation was very brief, too brief to be strained. He was at mom's getting his hair pressed and curled for his birthday party that evening. He joked about me being too to "well to do" and "holy" to come down to the bar and have a drink with him but, he understood and was happy I was happy and doing well. We laughed and I told him I loved him and hung up.

Hindsight is 20/20.

If I had any idea what was going to happen in the next 24 hours I would have raced across town to mom's place, told him I loved him and gave him a big, fat, wet kiss.

I was still selfish and I paid the conversation no more attention. I turned my attention to something more important, moving out of our current apartment.

When my husband and I returned to Milwaukee, we moved into an old bank that had been renovated into nice apartment. There were even a few prominent city officials living there. The problem was the building was on 3rd street, recently renamed Martin Luther King Dr. and North Avenue.

We all know where each major city has found fit to rename after Dr. King. Straight in the middle of the ghetto! So every night, no matter the weather, I went to sleep to the sound of sirens and quite frankly, I was sick of it.

My husband wanted to stay. The city was redeveloping that part of the city and he wanted to be right dab in the center of the action. He thought it was "retro". Everyone else thought so, why couldn't I see that he was giving me a better life that I had grown up with?

At the time he was the only person I knew more stuck up and in denial of his upbringing than me. We both had issues. But, he didn't want to move. And we often had heated "discussions" about it.

On this particular warm, Saturday night in mid-June, my husband didn't want to discuss anything remotely close to moving so; I sat and sulked the rest of the evening. When it was time to go to bed, I turned off the AC and opened the windows in my daughter and our bedroom. I hated being cold and could not sleep with it on. Our apartment was on the 5th floor so I didn't worry about someone creeping in on us.

I only said a prayer that I could make it through the night without being awakened by sirens. Unfortunately for me that prayer was not to be answered.

Around midnight, I really can't recall the exact time I was awakened because I don't remember looking at the clock, I heard a series of firecracker like sounds, followed a short time later by sirens. I knew from "experience" the popping noise was gunfire.

I turned over and told my husband firmly, "You are going to get us out of here, and there won't be any more discussion about it".

Then I cursed the siren, the people they were transporting and, I fell into a deep sleep.

Two in the morning my phone rang. I looked at the clock because the phone startled me but that didn't matter, I always answered my phone no matter the time. I still do. The caller ID said it was my mother.

She and I had begun to repair our relationship when my daughter was born and, since we'd move back to town she doted on her. I loved to see the two of them together. Not only did they look alike but they loved to be together as much as I loved watching them. I was happy and feeling secure again.

I was curious as to why my mother would be calling me at such an hour. My first thought was that something had happened with one of my uncles but, I didn't ponder it long, I just answered.

Sleepily I answered "Hello". The voice on the other line was eerily calm and controlled. I sat up.

"Stacy, Robert has been shot".

"Waaht?" I didn't fully grasp what she was telling me. "Is he going to be okay"?

There was a long pause, "yes", she answered.

"Okay mother, I'll call you in the morning" I replied.

"Okay baby, good night".

Now that was strange. My mother had never called me baby before. I shrugged it off and went back to sleep.

The next morning, as had been the tradition I resumed upon return to Milwaukee, I got up and prepared to go to church with the rest of my family. Mid-way through my shower I remembered the early morning phone call. I went to the phone and dialed my mother.

She didn't answer. I knew she was sitting there looking at the caller ID. She never went to church early. Still, I was confused. Then, I got scared. Was Robert really okay? I dialed my maternal grandmother.

She was the keeper of all family news. If something went down, she was the first one her sisters called. There was no answer there either. At any given moment, there were at least 4 people at my grandmother's house. Plus, on Sunday's uncle Mitchell came over early to bring her the newspaper. She was awake. But, why didn't anyone answer?

A cold chill ran through my body and I did what I had been avoiding. I called mom and daddy's house. The phone was off the hook. I knew this because it went straight to voicemail. Now, I was petrified. My brother was not okay. Someone answered that phone line 24 hours a day. This was not good.

I hurriedly explained the situation to my husband. He agreed to take the baby with him to his mom's house since he never went to church with us anyway. There he would wait for me to call.

I took the stairs down to the parking pad, too impatient to wait for the otherwise slow elevator. By the time I reached my little Renault Alliance, my legs felt like rubber. This couldn't be happening to me. I can't lose him, I just can't.

I cautiously drove to the other side of town to the Jenkins home because I was completely aware that something was horribly wrong but, not wanting to except it. As I pulled onto the narrow street I notice that all the way down the block there was no parking, on either side of the street.

Driving slowly, pretending to look for a spot to park, I saw my grandmother's car, then my Uncle Jerry's car. Wow, all of the great-aunts were there except the two still living in Mississippi. Daddy's car was even there. He should be in Sunday school.

Damn! Not Robert, not my brother. Damn! He didn't even get a chance to hold the baby. Quickly the selfishness of my decision hit me and hit me hard. But, I was still being selfish because my thoughts and worries were all about me. I came to a slow rolling stop in the middle of the street.

"FUCKKKKKKKKKKKKKKKKKKKKKKKKK! What had I done? Where's Robert" I screamed!

She knew! She knew he wasn't okay and she lied to me! I was once again angry with my mother and myself simultaneously.

I was angry with her for lying to me. I was not a child anymore. I could handle the truth! I should have been here shortly after she called. Here, at home with my family!

I was angry with myself because inside, I knew my mother hadn't told me because she knew how much I loved Robert and she didn't want me running out of the house in the middle of the night, feeling and acting like I was right now.

She was doing what she felt was the right thing to do for me. And, here I was angry and cursing her. Selfish, selfish, selfish!

I found a parking spot on the next block and walked back to the house. Inside all of the aunts were sitting in the living room. I knew from the pained look on everyone's face what happened. Robert was dead. But where was my mom and I didn't see daddy anywhere.

I spoke to those in my path on the way to her bedroom. Outside her door was Brianna. One look at me and she burst into tears. "Can I see momma?" I asked.

"Yes, but she's been sedated and probably won't know you're in there." I didn't care, I went in anyway.

She was lying on the bed with a folded wash cloth on her head. I leaned over and hugged her. "I love you" I said. She hugged me back really tight.

"I know baby, I know".When she released her embraced I turned and walked out of the room. She needed some rest and I had no idea what to say to her.

I was numb. But, I didn't want to be alone, so I went in the living room and sat down next to Aunt Bernice, the youngest of the great aunts. "How you feeling", she asked.

"I don't really know this is surreal. I can't believe he's dead. What happened?"

She looked at me as if she expected me to cry.

"He was at his birthday party on 29th and Walnut when he got a page from his girlfriend. He went outside to find a phone to call her back he was shot several times in the chest. He died in the ambulance on the way to Mount Sinai hospital".

My mind was really spinning now. 30th and Walnut is very near our apartment. And Mount Sinai is even closer. The sirens! Did I hear the ambulance taking my beloved brother to the hospital and curse it? No, I couldn't have but, I cursed someone, It could only be karma.

"What time, when did this happen", I needed to know.

"We don't know exactly yet, but it was sometime around midnight. And," she added "we think that bitch set him up. We're not sure yet but we WILL find out"!

Whoa, whoa, what bitch? Where she at? The hood was bubbling up inside of me with murderous intentions.

"Why do you think she set him up?" I further inquired.

"Well, her nickname is the Black Widow. Every man she has dated in recent years has been a drug dealer and every last one of them has been murdered."

NO! That couldn't be true. Robert would have known that type of information. He would have never allowed her to get close, I thought. But, I kept quiet.

I was practicing keeping my thoughts and emotions to myself and being observant. A lesson Robert tried to teach me when he was babysitting me and I was still a spoiled brat.

I now felt the need to recall every lesson he taught me and put them to use. I had a Black Widow to find. Yes, I was still not thinking right. But, she had taken something from me!

The aunts never act without getting all the information first. If Aunt Bernice told me this, it is because that is what she and her sisters believed based on contact information. And, if this is what the Aunts believed, it's what I should believe too. Family came first to them, no matter the circumstances.

Now, it was time for me to grow up and follow in their footsteps. Well, now it was time for me to at least grow up and stop living in my self-centered fantasy world.

I sat at the house for a long time. I didn't want to leave. I didn't want to be alone with myself. I wanted to displace my anger on the Black Widow. I didn't want to have to face the fact that now; it was too late to say I'm sorry and explanations. Too late to let my baby girl sit on his lap and feel the love I had felt for so long. Too late for hugs, wet kisses and long conversations and, it were much too late to seek his protection.

I felt I was really on my own now. But, I had to go home. I had a husband who was worried about me and needed to hear from me and, I had a daughter who needed me period. This was not a time to revert back to be a spoiled brat. It was time to be a grown woman and use the knowledge Robert gave me to avoid hazards and succeed in life.

These are the things I told myself on the long walk back to my car. It was time. Time to join the aunts and put family first, time to be a support for my family in need and, time to stop running from my demons and get on my knees.

I wanted to cry! My brother had been murdered, set up by a trick as bitch but, I didn't. But, the tears wouldn't flow.

My chest was tight and there was a knot in my throat but, I couldn't cry. I thought this is what hell must feel like.

On the ride back to my apartment my thought and emotions came in whirlwind like waves. I don't know how I made it home because I could see nothing but Robert's face.

He had a light skinned round baby face. He looked very much like Terrance Howard did in Dead Presidents. Watching him in movies makes me remember Robert, which is hard for me. And he's making a lot of good movies now.

The next morning, I followed my normal routine, dressing, dropping my daughter off at daycare and going to work. After work, I went straight to mom and dad's home.

Mom was still in bed and daddy nowhere in sight. There were less people there than the day before but, the living room was still crowded.

As, Aunt Bernice, Theresa, Brianna, my cousin Lisa and a few others sat around the living room talking softly, another cousin ran inside in a panic, stopping in the center of the room.

"Monica is outside trying to kill Bryson!" I pulled off my shoes and ran out the front door.

The previous night, I fought with my demons and didn't get much sleep. Dressing the next morning proved a little difficult because I hadn't prepared my work clothes at night as I normally do.

I had dressed quickly into a sundress, because it didn't need to be ironed and put my hair in a neat pony tail and bang. Being a petite young woman, this attire made me look younger than my 23 years.

When I arrived outside, there was a woman with a broken beer bottle threatening to kill Bryson. She was blocking his entrance to the house lunged at him when he got close.

Bryson was a small framed man, barely standing five feet tall and she wasn't much taller looking about five feet three. Of the three of us I was definitely the tallest at five feet seven but, I only weighed 125 pounds and *that* put us all on an even scale in a fight.

I sized her up quickly. I didn't know who this Monica was but, I didn't give a damn either. It was about to go down now, no introductions were needed.

How dare she come to a house in mourning and threaten another family member? She should have asked someone before making that decision.

I pushed her out of the way and stood between her and Bryson. Bryson, knowing the Calvary had indeed arrived began to taunt her while supplying me with important information.

"Bitch, you set my uncle now you about to get yours"!

"Mothafucka, I don't know what the fuck you talking about"! She yelled back. "But, you stole my shit and I want it back"!

"Bitch, I don't give a fuck who you are, but, you will not fuck with anyone here. Not today", I told her.

"Little girl, you need to mind your manners and stay out of family business".

You've got to be kidding me? She really didn't know did she? This was the tramp that we believed set Robert up, trying to hit Bryson with a broken beer bottle; I knew she really was only trying to create a scene with that weak mess but, my anger at who she was, and the fact that she was even here got the best of me. At the point of finding out her identity, I would have fought her on G.P.

"Take another swing with that bottle and you will find out just how young I am", I said.

Family members began to file out back door on the side of the house as Mom and Theresa walked down the front steps. Mom stood next to Theresa while she went to the wench and asked what was going on. As a small crowd gathered in the front yard, Monica started crying.

"Momma Jenkins, Bryson broke into my apartment and stole all my stuff" she cried.

Now, everyone in that yard knew she was lying. As soon as this bitch knew Robert was dead, she went back to the apartment they shared and completely emptied it out!

She had set him up but, we couldn't prove it. Later Aunt Bernice told me they were keeping her close, pending the murder investigation, because even the police knew of her reputation and thought she was involved.

After Theresa grabbed her by the shoulders and took her inside, Mom walked over and kissed me on the cheek then followed the other two and the crowd started to disperse.

Damn! I really wanted to fuck her up. But, I understood the situation. We'd have the opportunity to meet again. Milwaukee was too small for us not to.

Robert's wake was the following Friday. I went alone and early so that I could have some quiet time with him and hoping to finally cry.

When I approached the casket, the first thing I noticed was that his head was grotesquely large. And, I didn't remember him being that heavy set.

Then I looked down at his hands. His fingers were intertwined and folded peacefully, resting on his mid-section. But, his chest, he didn't have one. It looked as though his rib cage had been surgically removed or caved in.

I began to hyperventilate so; I sat down on a folded chair in front of the casket and tried to calm down. Initially, I wanted to talk to him. Tell him everything I had neglected to. But, I knew thought that was stupid.

Then, I wondered if his soul was in heaven. He had hurt and misled many people in his short life. But, I knew that God knew his heart. Yet, I wasn't sure if that was enough.

I didn't know what to do so, I just sat there remembering. And, the tears still didn't come.

The funeral was quite a dramatic event. When my husband and I arrived, Brianna was walking back and forth in front of the church with no shoes on crying. I hugged her tightly then went inside.

The church was full but, I was amazed that the pimps and whores he associated with were dressed reasonably well. No loud colors, wide hats, or miniskirts to be found.

Mom was upfront crying loudly and daddy was stiff and quiet. I wondered if Robert and dad had ever gotten a chance to repair their relationship or, if dad felt the same shame as I.

I sat up front with the great aunts. There were no husbands or tears allowed in this row. I was now considered a woman in the family.

Women in my family have suffered great losses emotionally, and wore them like badges of honor. It was my turn.

They knew that, even though no one that day would say it aloud, he was my brother and thought it strong and admirable that up until that point, I had not shed a tear so, let me in their circle of comfort.

At the repast, in the basement of the church, I served food to keep my thoughts clear of emotion and, I went through the entire event without shedding a tear. What was wrong with me? Why couldn't I cry? More karma I guess.

After the funeral, life for my family with only a few exceptions went on as normal. Alicia moved to Chicago, got married, and started her own family.

Bryson, who had dropped out of school and couldn't find a job, went to jail numerous times for petty theft and minor drug infraction. I guess he was trying to be like his now infamous uncle.

Theresa resumed her normal way of life but, she was hardly ever around anyway.

Thomas never kicked his habits. After his divorce, his life took a turn for the worse and he has been in prison ever sense.

Brianna, got drug treatment, completed nursing school to become a CNA. She eventually opened her own daycare. I love her so much and I am very proud of her. She will always be the most beautiful woman I know; inside and out.

But, mom, I don't think she has ever recovered. Pictures of Robert adorn every wall in her living room. She doesn't talk about him much anymore but, her eyes have never lost the pain.

I ran into Monica once. I was shopping with my best friend at the local G-Mart. We were laughing and talking about our upcoming camping trip.

After I emptied my cart onto the check-out counter I looked up and there she was ringing up my stuff! I just stood there looking at her.

She looked old and tired. And, not once did she look up at me, not even when she took my cash (I had immediately decided not to use a credit card).

I know she had to feel me staring at her. But, did she recognize me? All the anger, I had once felt, no longer carried the emotional intensity of the first time I saw her. And, I wanted it to!

I wanted to get angry all over again…and I couldn't. I didn't. I just grabbed my bags and walked out of the store.

Me, I went on with life as normally as I could. By the time of Robert's death I had established my own family and they were my priority. Still, every so often, feel the pain of my selfishness.

That part of me I have worked very hard to change. I never want to waste another moment of my life being selfish and, I treat others exactly like I want them to treat me, and I love hard, intensely; so, I have been told.

It is important to me now, to show people I love just how much I love them, unconditionally, whether they are ready for or can handle my intensity. I don't ever want another person in my life to not know exactly what they mean to me so, I give them me, completely, until they show that they are not worthy of that love, then I love them from a distance because real love is eternal, real love alludes death.

And now, each and every time I hear a siren, I pray. I pray that God allow the emergency personnel to make it to their destination safely and in time to do His will and the save the life of the person in need.

Blessed be the ties that bind.

Saving Grace

Exhausting is
This maze of
Life
Trying to figure out
The difference between
Wrong
And
Right
We sometimes
Stray
Onto
Paths
Into
Frays
And ruckus
That don't
Become
Us
Leaving others
Tired
And
Exhausted
Living in
Maybes
Mommas
Daddies
Abandoning their babies
Then wondering
Y
This world is
So
Crazy
Women
And
Men

Disregarding their
Souls
Raping
Each others
Minds
To achieve
What at best
Can be described
As
Lust
Redesigning
Morality to fit
None
Of
Us
But
Self
Spewing venom
At one another
For
Worthless
Wealth
Envious
Desires the
Greedy
Inspire
Believing
Our future
Is in dire
Need
Of
A
Revolution
Just because he is black
or
Just because she is white
And

Just because we have forgotten
How to
Enforce
Whats right
Redefining
Wrong
Into a pretty picture
Or a
Rap song
Cant be the way
To
Save
Me
U
Us
And them too
We need each other
Yet
We bleed each other
Of
The
Very
Life
We are all
Drowning
In
With
One another
Theres
No place
To hide
No where
To go
But
Share
Is a word
Very few

Of us
Know
The true definition of
Because
We
Just
Refuse
To
Grow
The way it is
Is all
We
Know
So much to prove
To those
We
Say
dont matter
Indulging in
Idle
Chatter
Regarding
Needless
Splattering
Of misdirected
Souls
Lost with us
In this maze
We
Know
As
Life
Still looking
For
THE ONE
To guide us
And make

Things right
Forgetting
To recall
The most important
Thing about
Us
That
JESUS
Already
Gave
HIS
Life!

Sex and Satan

…some say a lesson bought is a lesson earned….

Sex, enjoying life and her newly purchased freedom, received an email from Satan late one evening. In this email he described in detail his admiration for what he thought she endured. He said he studied her eyes, and lamented desire for her grace. He said he wanted to uplift her to her rightful place. But there was a catch; as with Satan there often is but, an email was not the place to make such a deal. So, Sex called Satan. At first there were only pleasantries exchanged. More compliments and phrases to help Sex relax and ease and become unrestrained. It didn't take long for Sex to become caught in the gallantry of Satan's lure.

"Submit to me" he said, "unconditionally". And, I will provide all your needs as you will belong only to me."

Submission was not a problem for Sex. She had submitted before. But, no one could have forewarned her of the pain she was about to endure…

"Will you submit to me"? Satan asked.

"Yes" Sex answered.

"Unconditionally"?

"Yes" Sex replied.

"Close your eyes."

Sex closed her eyes. Tensing at not knowing what would come next and excited by the same.

"Feel the strength of my hand rubbing your shoulders. I want to release all the stress of your day. Give me your pain", Satan urged.

Sex reveled in the fact that Satan wanted to take care of her. She closed her eyes and exhaled deeply.

"Do you feel me"? Satan again inquired.

"Mmmmmmmmm, yes", Sex answered.

"Good, now listen to me. I am going to take you places you've never been. You will achieve a level of commitment and love unimaginable to others. Only you are deserving of such wonders because you belong to me. I will supply all your needs and desires, as long as you submit to only me."

This sounded so good to Sex. All the things she had recently been through in the past, with other lovers left her emotionally drained. Yes, she deserved everything Satan had to offer! The submitting part would be easy, as long as he fulfilled his part of the deal. How foolish of Sex to think she could control Satan…

The sound of Satan's voice began to pierce the walls Sex had built around her soul. He seduced her with his words. His tongue entered her ear with a silky smoothness that stirred passions unknown before.

"Tell me you love me" Satan softly commanded.

"What?" Sex asked. Okay I don't even really know him and I'm supposed to love him?

"Complete submission allows no of questioning me or my request", "now do as I have asked and tell me you love me".

Sex, thinking she could fool Satan, thought to herself "I'll play along for now".

"I love you", Sex responded.

For the next hour Satan continued his seduction of Sex's mind. Her fondled her thoughts and caressed her heart until he could feel her melting on the other end of the phone.

"I have to go now" Satan crooned "but, I promise, I will always contact you at least once a day. I will never let your eyes close without first hearing my voice first, for you are mine now. An endeared part of me and I never want to be without you. I love you, I need you and now we are one."

Then, he hung up. Sex didn't realize she had just been seduced. She felt strange, empty, alone, and couldn't quite understand why, but she still felt she had control over the situation.

"Besides", she thought, "he's probably some lonely heart looking for a little phone sex". "I'll play along for a while", she thought again "this could be quite interesting".

If only she knew….

…Sex's bed, usually warm and comforting, draped in mounds of pillows, did not lull her to sleep that night. She tossed and turned for hours then, believing it was the temperature

of the room, Sex adjusted the heat and grabbed another blanket.

After a restless night, Sex awakened to the sound of her phone ringing. The caller ID read PRIVATE. Her first thought was to let the answering machine pick up was quickly vanquished by another, "it could be him".

"Hello" Sex answered.

"Good morning, did I wake you?" Satan greeted.

"No", Sex replied, trying to act as if she were already up and moving around. "I had just started to get ready for work".

The sound of Satan's sensuous laughter filled the room and soothed her restless spirit. "Silly" Satan quipped.

"You can't lie to me. I told you we are one now. Don't you feel me?"

Confused, Sex sat upright on the edge of the bed. I was too early for this psychosomatic crap. Yet, she was afraid say what she was really thinking so; she forced a "yes", to fall from her mouth.

"LIAR," Satan yelled into the receiver, "I told you, you can NOT lie to me!" Then his voice calmed.

"I need you to do something for me, will you?"

"Yes" Sex answered, still quivering from the sound of Satan's anger.

"Close your eyes and lie down on the bed."

Sex did as requested.

"Are you lying down?"

"Yes"

"Good girl. Now, I am kissing your forehead. Do you feel that?"

"Yess," Sex exhaled again.

"Now, I am kissing your neck. Do you feel that"?

"Yesss," Sex whispered. She was starting to feel him; his lips upon her, kissing her neck.

"Grab your right breast! Now, squeeze it gently. That's my hand touching you. I'm showing you how much I love you."

Sex, began to remove more of the barriers in her mind and sink into Satan's fantasy.

"Now, spread your legs. I want you to feel my hardness inside you. Mmmm, you feel soooo good. Do you feel me inside you? Giving you my love?"

"Yessssss!" He felt so good to Sex. So hard; soooo deep.

"Tell me you're my bitch!"

Sex's eyes popped open and she sat straight up! "Okay, now he's gone too far!"

"No, I can't do that," Sex yelled back!

"Say it!" Satan demanded.

"NO!"

"Then you are not ready for all that I can give you!" With that said, Satan hung up.

Sex sat on the bed for a few minutes. Happy no one was around to see how lost she looked. She actually felt lost. "What is going on with me", she thought. "Let me get my behind to work!" Still, she couldn't help but hope he would call back…

On the drive to work, Sex couldn't stop thinking about Satan. Who was really out of control her, him or her? She was too control to let anyone control her. She was well aware of what just the sight of her body did to men in intimate situations.

Why was Satan so appealing to her? Was it the intrigue of what he would say to her next? Was it because just the sound of his voice made her tingle and wet? "Damn, what is it?", she thought to herself.

At work, she found it hard to concentrate. She had a major case to prepare by the end of the day. Thoughts of Satan kept interrupting the process. By noon she was a wreck.

Even her co-workers commented on how strange and aloof she seemed. "Fuck it, I better go to lunch and regroup, besides" she thought, "he ain't going to call anyway, and I'll be damned if I call him again!" Just as she pulled into a parking space at the park, her cell phone rang. It was a PRIVATE call! Sex got excited and pissed off at the same time. "I can't believe…Shit, let me get this"!

"Hello", said Sex trying to sound calm.

"I missed you, and I'm sorry I reacted so harshly toward you. Will you forgive me"?

"Wow, um, yeah." Sex tried to sound forceful and in control when she made her next statement.

"Don't ever talk to me that way again"!

"I won't, I promise. I…I, just became so angry at the thought of you not being completely mine. Not surrendering the way you said you would. I…I love you. And, I want us to be one forever".

"How could you feel that way about me so soon" Sex replied. "We don't even really know each other, we just met, and we haven't met physically. So, you can't honestly feel that way."

"I said I love you, I'm not in love with you yet".

Sex said she understood but, she didn't. She just didn't want him to hang up. She was feeling a need, if for nothing else the sincerity in his voice. It made her want him deeply. But, Sex needed that physical contact to be sure she really wanted him.

"I want you see you" Sex stated.

"Close your eyes"

"No," said Sex, "not that way. I want you physically feel you".

"And you will my Love, but until then, I need you to close your eyes, pleeease".

"Well", Sex thought, "he did say please".

"Are they closed"?

"Yesss", Sex whispered.

"What are you wearing"?

Sex started to end the conversation but, as is said by many, curiosity killed the cat. On this day that statement would prove most profound.

"I'm wearing a skirt and blouse" Sex replied.

"Are you wearing stockings"?

"yyyes".

"Take them off"!

"I can't do that, I'm in a public park"!

"Okay, then I guess this conversation is over, I'll call you later".

"No wait" Sex said with a sense of urgency. "I'll do it".

"Are they off"?

"Yes"

"Good girl. Now, lie back in the seat and close your eyes; let me know when they are closed".

"They're closed".

"I love you, and until we can be together physically, this is how I'm going to make love to you. But, you can only feel me by submitting to me, do you hear me"?

"Yesssssss" Sex moaned.

"Now reach down into your panties and rub your clit".

Sex did as she was instructed. But, that request was only the beginning. For the next hour Satan whispered, moaned and cajoled Sex to think things she never would have imagined. She climaxed over and over again in the park. Never giving a thought to who could be watching.

Satan was getting close to taking completely control of Sex. But, today he had his fill.

"Did you cum?" he asked.

"Of course," Sex swooned.

"Good girl. I told you, submitted and I will take you to new heights in life and love. I have a meeting to get to now but, you will hear my voice again tonight, I promise".

When the call ended, Sex opened her eyes and immediately became embarrassed. There was no one around, no one watching but, she looked around just to be sure.

Once sure no one was around, she started up the car and drove off. Sex felt so liberated! She'd never done anything even close to this freaky before, what a milestone. She felt too exuberant to go back to the office. So, called her supervisor, gave a flaky excuse about getting a flat and waiting for AAA then drove home to wait for Satan's next call....

Satan's seduction of Sex went on like this every day for three months.

Sex had become dependant on hearing Satan's voice, at least once a day. She was on cloud nine and felt beautiful but, her once vibrant and sexy appearance was anything but that. Her hair, at the beginning of this affair was long, soft and beautiful. Now, it had a dry, stringy look to it and had begun to break.

She no longer went to work looking polished from head to toe but, was wearing jeans, sneakers on a regular basis. Her productivity at work had dropped dramatically also, and the house was a train wreck!

Sex, noticed none of these changes. All she could understand was Satan's voice gave her life new meaning. Even church became a thing of the past. How could she go to church and risk missing a call from Satan?

One morning Sex received an unusual call. When the phone rang she was lying in bed waiting for Satan's call. But, instead of PRIVATE, the I.D. said UNKNOWN. She answered anyway because it could still be Satan.

"Hello", Sex murmured. Ready for her morning fix.

"How are you Beautiful?" the caller asked.

"I'm good", said Sex was now irritated because it clearly wasn't Satan. He never called her beautiful.

"I miss you" the caller said. His voice was deep and very low, almost like he was whispering, and even more soothing than Satan's.

"Who the fuck is this"? Sex was becoming more irritated because it wasn't Satan and someone was clearly playing games with her.

"Come back to me, I can give you your life back", and then the caller hung up.

Sex was shook. She didn't know what to think but, dismissed it merely as a prank call. She sat on the edge of the bed for a couple minutes more then went to the bathroom to shower before work. Praying Satan didn't call while she was away from the phone.

When she turned on the light in the bathroom she caught a glimpse of her face in the mirror. "Wow", she said, noticing the bags under her eyes. "I've got to get more sleep".

She showered and dressed. Paying close attention to the caller I.D. each time she re-entered the bedroom. Satan had not called. "I guess", she thought, "I have time to curl my hair this morning". All day at work, Sex kept checking her cell phone. Still no call from Satan, nor did he call her that night.

The next morning, the phone rang and Sex hopped out of bed to answer it, grabbing it without looking at the caller I.D..

"I love you more than you love yourself" the voice on the other line said, "Come back to me". Then he hung up again.

"Damn crack-head" Sex yelled as she hung up the receiver. Satan did not call at all again that day.

This went on for a week. Sex received a call from the UNKNOWN caller every morning. Each day he professed his love for her and requested she come back to him. At first not hearing from Satan worried Sex.

She felt herself slipping into a depression but, tried to counter act it by using the time to do her hair, nails, toes and clean her house.

By the end of the week she was almost back to the way she was three months ago. Then the inevitable happened.

Friday evening, just as she was about to settle down with a book, the phone rang. PRIVATE call…It was Satan.

Sex felt her heart jump with excitement but, something inside her told her not to answer it. Surprisingly she didn't. She decided to walk to the store for some juice, and left her cell phone behind.

When she returned, she had missed six PRIVATE calls and one UNKNOWN call. The UNKNOWN caller was the last call and had left a message.

"I want you back, please listen to me, I can give you your life back". That was all he said. Sex had become used to his statement. She quickly erased it, turned off the ringers on both phones and read until she fell asleep.

The next morning, Sex, who was still sleeping on the couch, was awakened by the phone. She knew she had turned off the ringers last night but, how was it now ringing and, who was it?

Sex, still in a daze jumped up. As she grabbed for the house phone, her cell phone rang.

"What the HELL is going on" she spoke aloud. Sex, grabbed her cell phone off the coffee table when her answering machine clicked. "Don't answer that"! The caller said, and then hung up. Her cell phone stopped then started ringing again.

This time she was able to look at the caller I.D.. It was a PRIVATE call. Now the house phone was ringing.

Sex ran to look at that caller I.D. just as the cell phone stopped ringing, it read UNKNOWN. "ok", Sex spoke out loud again, I am really losing my mind!

The voice on the answering machine was more forceful than it had ever been before.

"Don't answer that, come to me, I can give you your life back", CLICK!

The cell phone had begun to ring incessantly. I wouldn't even go to voicemail, it just kept ringing. Sex was scared really now, she didn't know what to do. She was standing in the middle of the room holding the vibrating, ringing cell phone and listening to another message from the UNKNOWN caller.

"You know what to do, come back to me"!

With both phones ringing in her ear, Sex began to feel faint. Just as she began to slide downward a voice yelled out to her "Come to me! Open the door, and come to me, I will save you"!

Sex willed all back as much strength as she could muster and started to crawl towards the door. When she pulled up on the doorknob to stand a very familiar voice rang in her head.

"I love you, I need you, and we are one"!

"Satan", Sex yelled! "Oh my God, what is going on"?

Then she heard "Hurry, open the door, I'm right outside, I will save you".

Sex turned the knob. Just as she swung the door open, there was a loud clap, then a flash of bright light! Now on the verge of insanity, Sex opened her mouth to scream just as a hurricane gust of wind moving from the back of the house shoved her out the opened door into her apartment hallway and slammed her into the adjacent wall. Sex slid to the floor unconscious.

When Sex awoke, her eyes focused on her apartment door, hanging from its hinges.

"What in the world," Sex wondered quietly. She pulled herself up to resting on her knees and her eyes were diverted to something lying on the floor in front of her, a gold chain with a tiny pedant. Sex picked up the chain to examine the pendant. It glimmered then, it flashed. As it flashed lights began to go off in her head.

Each flash showed a scene from the last three months. Her deterioration, her deception by Satan, loss of self was revealed to her. When the flashes stopped, Sex again looked at the pendant swinging on the chain in her hand. It was a small Crucifix…

Sex began to cry and moan as if she was in pain. "Thank-you Jesus, thank-you Jesus", she said over and over again. A neighbor and his girlfriend walked in the hallway. Sex saw them and began to laugh and eerie laugh. She looked her neighbor straight in the eye and yelled "THANK-YOU JESUS", at the top of her lungs.

"I'm okay", she said to her neighbor, "now".

But, Sex didn't stop laughing. She'd seen what she had become and, Jesus had delivered her from the deception of Satan on this day and now, she would concentrate on loving Him and herself as they both deserved to be….

Sex and Satan the Discussion

Okay, I know you all are thinking, "This chick has issues'. But, I had something to say.

Without just coming out and telling you, I wanted you to think about it first.

I could have called the female in this story by any of todays or yesterdays for that matter, vices. She could have been call Heroin, Alcohol, Crack or even "Weed". But, we all know, SEX SELLS! (LOL)

An addiction of any kind is no worse than another. Sort of like sin. No one sin is greater than another...

Sin is sin, wrong is wrong. But, through the acceptance of Jesus Christ as our Lord and Savior we, can overcome ANYTHING! This is just one woman's opinion.

Please don't any of you non-believers in Christ send me mail 'cause I just ain't above cussing you out. If you don't like what's being said, replace Christ with whom or whatever you believe in and see if it still applies; if it doesn't, again, don't send me any hate mail cause I ain't above cussin' you out.

We all backslide now and again ;)!

Okay, I'm tripping, send me what you like. But, I don't have to respond, how's that? You still might get cussed out but, life is about choices!

Stay Blessed,

The1Essence

The Next Exchange

My body still tingles in the
places you touched
My mind often mingles with the memories of such
Although passion is not the only pleasure shared
with you
it is the one and only emotion that stands true
There are no subtle reminders of whence you came
Only resounding emotion laden memories
that patiently waits
for the next exchange

HE

She held my hand
While we walked
Through my fantasies
With the depth of her
Intense emotions
Se loved me
Made loved to me
Mentally
She changed the path of my existence
I wanted to inhale her
Bet the thought of
Exhaling
Almost
Crippled me
I felt helpless
In her
So I rebelled
Against her
Love
Instead of
Reveling in it
I pushed away
Instead of pulling her closed
I starved
Her hungry heart
And she
Disappeared
Now
I can not
Breathe

Smile

Hold me
Tightly
Squeeze me
Softly
Touch me
There
Feel me shiver?
Do it again
Watch me
Quiver
Look into my eyes
What does your mind
See?
Gently
Brush your lips
Against my cheek
save me
from myself
because it's
lost
in the excitement
of you
don't just read me
Listen closely
Do you hear what my
Heart is really saying
To you?

No Apologies

Your smile
Is so
Deadly
It traumatizes
My nervous
System
So
I cant look
At you now
For it
Will prolong
The
Evitable
Is here
Now
No
Apologies
Offered
To refuse
Giving you
My heart
Could
Never be
A mistake
You giving
Your heart
To
Him
Was
Catastrophic

Reachin'

In my dreams
I see your
Hands
Reachin' out
To me
Stroking my
Cheek
Caressin my
Chin
Lifting three fingers
Signing
You are my
Friend
Desiring
So much more
My eyes
Behind the
Lids
Explore
The possibility
Of your
Hands
Making my
Dreams
Reality

Really Real Reality

I'm mystified and
captivated
at the same time
by the way
you've captured
my heart
and completely
occupy my mind
If my feelings could
stand alone
and speak on their own
they'd speak on
how grateful I am
you've made my heart
your home
Sometimes
I swear not
I wonder
if you are really there
really real
not makebelievablly
making me happy
returning love
that transcends time
Then I remember
the lesson that taught me
to just be
not living for the moment
but
living in the moment
So
once again
I exhale
And
continue to live
in the reality

Passion

I need
U
Not
Just
Mentally
Deep inside
My flower
No longer
Budding
With the thought
Of being your
Freak
Spreading
My
Legs
Wide
Exposing
My wanting
Covered
In our
Explosion
Of wetness
Soiling
Sheets and
Minds
Of others
Aroused by
Our
Passion
Envisioning
thrusts
my
Moans
created by
love within you and me

Promise Me

Are you just as
Afraid
Of me
As I am
Of you
Please say it
I need
To hear your
Fears
Because
I am a
Nurturer
To my core
I desire
To take your
Cares
And make them
Free
Just promise
Me
One thing
You'll never
Ever
Lie
To me

I WISH

I saw a shooting star and I made a wish
for happiness.
I found a four leaf clover and I made a wish
for good health.
I saw a rainbow and I made a wish
for love.
I stood under an upright horseshoe and
i made a wish
for wisdom.
I thought I had everything I wanted and needed
In this lifetime,
But, I was not happy
Yet, I don't worry about my fiancés
And I am wise enough to know
How to live physically healthy
then
I went to church
I saw a crucifix
and fell on my knees
I cried
and I prayed
to be in love
with the man
I love

Music for Us by Us

U and I
Together
Create a symphony
Known to few
Desired by many
Understood by
None
It belongs to
Us
And there's no
Rush
To complete
It
That way
It stays
Unique
Not able to be
Repeated
By
Any
We live in it
We laugh in it
Constantly growing
In its
Many colors
And
Instruments
Drawing fulfillment
From the sound
Of the
Love
We are making

Hide-n-Seek

The wind is blowing
hard
In my face
Trying to slow me down
I keep running
fighting the wind
and you
I can't stand in one place
don't want you to
find me
Continually begging
my soul
to hide me
you said you only
want to
make me
happy
but my fear
of the unknown
has grown into a
to paranoia
I can't control
U want to
hold me
close
leaving notes
and a single
rose
Every where
Any where
if you think
I'm there
and when
you are
94
I'm not
My heart

has betrayed me
before
and is
desperate
to do it once more
so,
I've locked it away
And,
until you find me
I'll keep running

Circles

Is it too much to ask for a man
to want to know more about a
woman
than how her SEX feels?
If it is,
Then I know it would be too much
for a man to show that chivalry is
not dead and
true love is real
I mean
I know
These days
It's all about games
fuck for awhile
and never give a real last name
It's a shame
Never-the-less
There are rules to every game
And some women are as
thoughtless
as some men these days
Don't wanna be called ho's
but spread their legs to the lowest
bidder
and a crook
Quick to pull a bait and switch
then run and publish that dumb
shyt
in a book
Damn!
The old ways
Seem a long ways
forgotten
This world is one big circle
of how much
can be ill gotten
Swiftly

like we can take that shyt with
us
When Karma calls
to proclaim us all
victims

IF

If
Time stood still
For
Fate
I would have
No other choice
Left
But
To
Entice your
Soul
To visit
My
Space
Fulfilling
Your
ever most
Desired fantasies
Conquering
Your heart
With
Submissive
Grace
Leaving
No stone unturned
Yet
Nothing
Out of place
Only
My kiss
On your lips
If
Time stood still
For fate

DAMN IT!!

You tease me
Relentlessly
Vocalizing my thoughts
And believe me
I want to shout at you
Touch me!
Breathe me!
Love me!
Please me!
But,
That camera you've placed in my mind
Readily
Shares with the world
All that I think
We should be
Without even
Recognizing
Me
In the credits

Long Distance Lovers

Separate thoughts
using
one mind
Distant embrace
occupying an
intimate place
necessitating a
madding pace
to
fill an
empty
space
abandoning grace
in order to
deny fate
its control over
our destiny
We
awkwardly
defy odds
moving mountains
rapidly
rejecting those
who undoubtedly
want to be
U
and
Me
yet choose to
distort our
distinguished journey
through life
in love
with love
as merely
a
spree

nevertheless
we
persevere
Silencing
callous jeers
admirably
loving in
life
despite
the miles
between
us

Remembering

I am trying to forget
the embrace
that briefly let my
mind and heart call a truce
and enjoy the moment
I am trying to forget
the soft kisses
raining across my face
and down my neck
that swept
all negative thoughts away
into a soft pink and purple haze
I am trying to forget
the gentle hands
making wet
spaces long dry
I am trying to forget
sensuous bass
in words dancing around my ear
that convinced my body to
surrender a place
I had long neglected
I am finding it difficult to forget
because I so easily remember
every minute
(pressing my thighs together)
and re-living it
with tender affection
Savoring every second
of the feeling
a tongue made
as it deeply entered by psyche
(Damn)

I can still hear you
And thinking this way
there is no longer a need to forget
You see
you were right
"you had me".

Other books
By
The1Essence

Reflections of Light

Sunset, The1Essence of Life

Memoirs of an Ordinary Woman, Volume I

www.ingramcontent.com/pod-product-compliance
Lightning Source LLC
Chambersburg PA
CBHW060807050426
42449CB00008B/1583